Sarah Windebank

MEMORIES OF A SWEDISH GRANDMOTHER

myriad

First published in 2020 by
Myriad Editions
www.myriadeditions.com

Myriad Editions
An imprint of New Internationalist Publications
The Old Music Hall, 106–108 Cowley Rd,
Oxford OX4 1JE

First printing
1 3 5 7 9 10 8 6 4 2

A CIP catalogue record for this book
is available from the British Library

ISBN (pbk): 978-1-912408-48-1
ISBN (ebk): 978-1-912408-49-8

Designed by WatchWord Editorial Services, London
Typeset in Dante by www.twenty-sixletters.com

Printed and bound in Great Britain
by CPI Group (UK) Ltd, Croydon CR0 4YY

To my mum, Inger, and my sons, Joe and Max

Contents

Memories of a Swedish Grandmother

In a Baltic-blue work bib, she held me close
in her horny hands. She boiled, steamed, brewed—
                                                    hefted
her polished pans. She proved, then plaited weave
into rye bread, learnt from the loom's warp and weft.
My star-girl belly bulged with saffron bun
at winter's festival of light—sill, pear
in dill-smudged earthenware—while *Mormor* spun
me supple-strong, straight as a shining spear.

A thought of her Norse-inflected pidgin
returns me, spellbound, to a lisp-lipped kid;
small alien—two tongues fighting—polite
but insistent, through my dark-eyed head. My kin?
Angles, Swedes, I ravelled centos with them, skidded
the margins, planted seed—the wish to write.

University Library

after Theodore Roethke

The shuffle of shoes in the silent zone
takes me back to the playground sounds
of children moving in crocodile lines on concrete,
I in a dress—in the no-trousers-squad for girls—
that caused my thighs to freeze, my knees
to bleed from stumbles. The school nurse trowelled
gravel from my wounds at the old school sink,
then iodined me, with steely hands
and iron hair—watched by me, wide-eyed.
                                        Computerised
archives, wood box files, piles of papers,
excess, mucilage, pulped, bottled Resinol,
and dry debris, duly catalogued
by fossilised librarians; one wonders
now how girls got to libraries at all.

The Girl on the Allotment

Hot-dry root-rich pitch of the earth
on tangled plots betokens sun,
and chalk-marl soil in the fish-weed wind
creates a pungent loam, a joy.
She digs—soil stains her corduroy coat
and flies plot long in the lazy spring.

Leaf fronds furl greenly and shoots spring,
and she with her pitchfork digs the earth,
waters the pink bean flower, its coat
blossoming in the thin salt sun,
her damp nose sniffing garlic, as joy
jumps in her in the brackish wind.

The sea, silver swell, swirls a wind
inward with the tide—Taurus spring-
tide in the May storm of seeds. Joy
of harvest promised and the earth
breath passing through her form—the sun
now burns her neck, her back. The coat

removed and slung, it billows to coat
some neighbouring marguerites. Wind
it up, hand it back, she says, sun

in her dazzled eyes: make spring
my oxeye daisies from the earth.
She looks quite mediaeval, Joy

her name—and she says it's a joy
to wear a real gardening coat
streaked with alkaline soils and earth;
spy a coney's cottontail wind
down a warren, its long hind legs spring
into darkness under the turning sun.

A honey bee, the colour of the sun
and a black-eyed pea, its drone a joy
while she plants seeds, sucks the dewy spring.
Her sheltering wimple hat and coat
she dons to till a fine tilth; wind
keen, beating her still on the earth.

Joy hoes clods in her corduroy coat,
buds sup sun in the bullish wind,
and oxeyes spring from the seedy earth.

The Gift

is woven roughly
with the ridges and bulges
of a ploughed field
or cotton chenille.
It smells of unopened
drawers and talc.
It tastes of things
that may have been spilled—
lapsang souchong
or schnapps—
and is soundless,
unless she strokes
it against her peachy cheeks
and its susurration
sighs her own whisper,
or my memory of it.
The one word that haunts
the gift's day is *Mormor*,
its only thought the loom
it was woven on;
nothing so intense has happened
since its creation.

This dreamy discus reflects on fingers
caressing its gauzy threads,
yet shrinks from vases of Linnaea
borealis twinflower
that weigh its roundness down
and stain.
This place mat senses I am similar
to Grandma,
and would like to have companions—
a whole set of six.
It would like to multiply,
become a part of the family,

                                  be one with us.

Nettles

A spangle of jade fronds stings my hands
when, tramping over barren ground, I gather
lightweight ferns, that shift like things windborne.
They are a green invading force that overwhelms
cast-off cans, glass jars and old sacks,
returning the earth to its origins.

From a micro worm's view basal leaves gleam
ochre from loam, the upper tips striped malachite
struck with sunlight—but from my ambling bird's-eye
                                                    view,
I see a verdant, tropical sheen and a green cathedral
                                                    roof.

Stippled with stinging hairs
that prick the nerves and pink the veins,
it'll take a heft of dock to cool my skin.

I boil them and create a wilt of steam,
and make a soup, as good as spinach
to replenish and renew me, though a vagrant meal.

Pastoral

In our time of innocence, we sported naked
in the garden, to Marlene Dietrich
discs, blue lamp blues, while your father painted
his pregnant wife in the shadows
behind the French windows,
Arcadia, the bohemian emblems of suburbia,
the age of iron receding in a crescendo
of golden masks and dragons.

I visited you once in your barn home, Colossus,
your face a swirl of blue paint,
and driving down to Brighton in a pink Beetle
we made small talk; a grace and splendour
radiated through the hum of the motor.
There, we spoke to a guy on a bike about *Comus*,
outside the pier show.

Later, you compromised and joined the Greens:
life became polemic and meetings in church halls.

Yet now, you are an artist,
a commedia dell'arte performer.
You tour Italy and Edinburgh,

festive behind a masque of swozzles,
Scaramouche, swathe of silk shifts,
and green crocodiles.

But in a simpler time, the laburnum
shading chaise longue and cello,
the grey rocking horse swaying in the still hallway,
two children were transported to the
nineteen-thirties:
you were Eliot, I Auden, in a once-in-a-lifetime
confrontation, in which I suffered, but won.

At a Bus Stop in Kemptown,
on Saturday Night

You would sneak up behind a beauty
in leather jacket with cropped hair,
put your hands over her fine eyes
and say, I love you;
watch the shaven-headed men waltz
with linked arms in the balmy night.
Two women passed like adolescent boys,
scooting side by side in hoodies and wide jeans
in soft star sneakers, their hair
identical crops, spiky, copper-coloured
like brown mouse pelts,
with a look of sweet undercliff skaters.
You wondered if they huddled
in white mansions by the sea
and cavorted lovingly.
Gay men eyed you as a friend: you looked like them.
I'm butch but delicate all-in-one, you said.
Pale passion took you as you stood
at a bus stop in Kemptown.

Lupi, Ursi, and Other Smaller Beasts

I adore wild beasts, like less-domesticated ones.
The smell of peaty soil on English rain-soaked
mornings ripples through me like light on lakes,
and I remember transatlantic animals and hills,
waterfalls tinted flax by widening skies.

Wolves were fine-fleshed and skeletal
in Canada, they lived off the land. Lupine
cadaverous, they died young, starved frozen.
But in Toronto, in ordered gardens,
chipmunks abounded, black squirrels foraged,

and raccoons ranged noisily through household bins.
Orienteering north, I met a male and female
moose heading south, with slow pedantic
ploughing of the roadside verge, and there were fox
                                                    cubs
too, gambolling their short life away, begun in spring,

and not yet knowing petrifying winter
that would kill them in their prime. Black bears
uprooted trees in the Algonquin, once Inuit
tracks and trails, and the star-nosed mole
marked the rooty forest paths with scat.

Dams, abandoned lakes and the scarred gnawed
                                        landscape
of beavers vanished as I drove back to Toronto,
to the Metro Zoo, and watched the polar bears
through a subterranean glass panel, like icy yeti
floating aqueously, distilled in amber light.

Women Sewing

My mother leaks quaint tales like sappy bark,
queer yarns that stitch themselves into my heart,
knitting the past—of serfs and atavistic aunts
whose traces touch my skin like breath on glass.
Here, in my wooden home, rubbed in, embossed
on flinted floors, ruts, symbols of the lost:
pure parabolas carved by felt-shoed agility,
by girls who fashioned lace, its frangibility

like snowstorms, broken young, snapped short
                              Benighted
by graft and dim moonlight, the children boozed
all day on kvass, and soon their lives outran
the course of Chronos: the shadows and wan
stone of age ingrained like dried-out wood,
but still they sewed, like *noble* peasants should;
no crass commercial wares produced en masse,
but rare and worked, crafted with a stiff distaff

that had been carved with field and farmyard scenes
with great finesse, and rubbed till the birch
                              gleamed.

Babushka—all my kin—would stoke the hearth
to chase the icicles; serfed, hair bound in scarves,
skipping their hands over the threads lightly,
words hissing, smoke-like, slyly; white lies, white
                                        miles.
But as air ebbed to spring, the room's snow seal
                                        dissolved.
With children languorous, the moss-grown walls
                                        were warmed.

Islington

My friends made a home of a mossy basement flat
of depth and darkness, but open-hearthed, in Upper
                                                Street;
they foraged for firewood on Highbury Fields.

In philosophic moods, I would incline there,
brooding on tropes and Nathalie Sarraute,
and here we read and wrote our dissertations

for tutors sequestered in Bloomsbury squares.
We cycled through Islington and Kensington—
too young to care for finery or filthy lucre—

haunted Hackney and Newington Green,
in hopes of boys and thrills. Pursing
purple lips that gleamed like pearls,

we dressed in swirls of cheap silk creasing
and tumbling from a costumier's chest
that a sword carrier had raided from the Almeida.

Memories fly away like birds: when Arsenal
won the FA Cup and red and white-
striped scarves bedazzled Balls Pond Road,

but Canonbury Square was quiescent, buttoned-up,
and Aberdeen Park, my father's boyhood home,
stiffer still, unmoved by the display.

Some fusty, red-backed books, made by the Left
Book Club, were bought by Dad—a fellow traveller
then, now Labour-Party agent with his pipe and
                                                      papers—

and I read all I needed to of Rosa Luxemburg
and *Ann Veronica*, chewing on brown rice,
a candle sizzling on a cracked saucer, while Pa,

with his soft North London voice, taught
me about the Chartists, Cable Street
and what I ought to do; just ashes now.

Penelope Poem (1)
Abortion

after Sylvia Plath's Winter Trees

Her barque had foundered on the black rocks
of no hope. Childless,
she reflected upon a red womb
and herself enclosed,
Penelope weaving intestinal shrouds.

He left her in flux. Overcome
by social workers and debts,
she clutched on to the carcass
of her home and a girlfriend
with a daughter and herself to succour.

Now, looking back to the detritus,
crossing the water, nothing is internal.
Knowledge harnesses to a world
that is earthbound, flat, discrete,
and she canters then floats free to the tranquil sea.

Penelope Poem (2)
The Son

The woman wakes alone, half-blind, to sew:
she fashions fleeces—piecework—in the factory.
Her son ignores her now she's reached forty.
He learnt this from his dad, and all *he* sees
is an ageing bird—lips, legs, breast, waist and tum—
and *he* collects the boy on Saturday.
Did Telemachus ever talk to his mum?
I mean *talk*.
           He never bothers to embrace
the visionary sewing, and say that her passion
has breastfed him for five thousand years,
that the crosses she sews are gravestones,
that the circles above are halos, fashioned
symbols of women, or that the lashing pinking shears
must sever the umbilical thread with oedipal moans.

London Zoo

My son loved Birdman, not Spider-Man,
gazed at the parrots, pelicans and flamingos

in London Zoo, used to watch the keeper fill
his bucket full with fish, and flip them into the
                                        birds' bills,

until he spotted that his feathered favourites never
                                        flew
as they do in David Attenborough films.

Were they so unenchanted by the London scene,
so incurious about the world beyond the barbed
                                        wire fence?

And then he learned their wings were clipped and
                                        raw,
and they were hobbled aviators who hopped in pain

around a pen, true descendants of the limusaurus,
a beaked and feathered beast that never flew.

Autumn in Preston Park

The statues of two Roman boys by the Rotunda
are draped in golden leaves and fading roses,
as children dredge the pond for frogs and newts.

As autumn falls in clusters of acorn
and thorny blackberry, my body
near its year's end, like a leaf, withers and fails.

The frost that whitens the playing field
calcifies my thoughts in turn,
but I still play the grey middle ground.

And soon the scene is speckled with the twins'
red and green pom-poms that bounce madly
up and down in the keen wind—

flesh of my flesh, poles apart
yet hand-knitted together, in a way.

Daughter as Potter

I always remember my mother's hands
because she had arthritis: she worked hard
and suffered for it. *My* tremulous palms slide
over the grey earth, with a slap of my feet
on the floorboards—back and forth—
to the kiln. A spray of dust makes
my hair turn, momentarily pukka,
into a white plumage, like my mother's
flapping wings nestled about her pink ears—
pale blue-eyed bird with scratching, ersatz
economical tropes; having to boil barleycorn
for *pölsa*, but longing to ride the horse-drawn
plough that sowed a similar seed.
But *Mormor* nursed my prodigious need,
and interceded as I sat uncared for, mud-smutty
in a garden sandpit, in a dream of fairies and pee,
while she—with sapphire eyes—saw how it ought
                                        to be,
in her soft wool clothes and maroon felt hats. She
                                        crafted
and then beat the loomed rugs on the overarched
line to rout the dust—swish, swish, swish, swish—

thin form now hugged, gran's *liten flicka*
making witches' castles, other worlds from sand
that carried me away to distant lands.
Perhaps that spectral strand was the grown-up
world:

my inner child breaks out sobbing and I ape
myself, like a cankered cherry tree's bark,
withering and decaying to a lurid and ugly
present. So now, tough, thickset men as tall as trees
swear blind and raze my speckled golden sandpit
to the ground, knocking the heart out of a finer
world—

a social democratic, not a capitalist time.
And now, I sit in psychiatrists' rooms—
Mamma's barn, not one of her tragic loons.
It's sad how *hennes liten barn* grew up.
I fling the dense slippery mass
on to the wooden board. Like a foetus
aborted, it slides out—
dumped by men in green into yellow
bins—or like the mud at the low
point of a quick stream down a mountainside.
The dusty terracotta pots are fired
with slip, swirled round and coated
with a glaze. I throw a bulbous bell jug

blown this way and that on to the wheel,
and work my foot industriously.
It wings stiffly between my hands. I root
out air bubbles, begin again.
The bulging form swells then swings
in at the throat, tight like a noose round the rim
in graceful half chokes kicking
the air. My hands are creased with slurry. Cries
slice into the dusk until the last light dies
and I'm frozen in my activity,
stilled by the chilling night. Complete.
My nails are snapped from labouring, my hands
                                      chapped
but broad and flat from rubbing and twisting the earth.
They rest, quiescent on my aproned lap
that's smocked and tied with string around my waist.
Mor, Moster, Mormor—generations—
once sowed the corn, and sewed and weaved patience
into daughters' futures. My hands now ply
my craft and trade in a clay argot
from past tears to potter poet.
The pot and pen won't lie.

Swedish Santa Lucia Party

'Tis the yeare's midnight, and it is, the dayes,
Lucie's, who scarce seaven houres herself unmaskes,
*   The Sunne is spent, and now his flasks*
*   Send forth light squibs, no constant rayes'*

—*from 'A Nocturnall Upon S. Lucie's Day, being the shortest day'*
by John Donne

Shadows that signify an untrue solstice
                                    lengthen into Sagittarius
and darken the staircase on which the children
                                    will soon clamber.
The winter sun that sets at three
                                    is a marshmallow on fire,
and a dish of heart-shaped cakes is scented
                                    with cyanide
from almonds buttered into the ginger's heat.
The children yearn to pull the kernels out,
to savour the rough husk of the nut
and cry philippina when two drupes
                                    are descried,
and keep one, give one to a mate—
small players in a world of make-believe.

The house is warm with children
                              but there is no warmth,
only the hoar frost of a winter day.
And still, downstairs, the saffron buns
go fast, and star boys in their cardboard hats
and girls knotted in angel robes with candles
                              in their hair
sing Santa Lucia to the wooden rocking mare
who tries to ride on iron springs from chill
                              and into spring,
with coaxing mothers playing violins,
and the children safely gathered in,
but outwitted by the witching time.

Gap Year

Alone abroad and sixth form rules
just a few weeks' memory away,
she tried to settle into French country ways,
and would catch her breath at golden eagles
in the sultry air that reeked of heat and heather.
And at odd times, she'd appear as a complex shadow
in the village square, then drift down to the river.

There, she would bind a clutch of rosemary twigs
                                        into her hair,
and note the vines in stony fields that stretched
                                              away
to coils in purple scrub, which knotted her in plant
                                          and fibre.
The sun's distinct and varied light just pierced the
                                        chlorophyll,
changing her hue to match the green,
a young goddess of plants and innocence,
and so, the villagers named her their child, or
                                        la vierge.

A year later, a History undergraduate
ensnared reluctantly in a London pub,
her masks a black leather jacket and roll up,
Marx and dialectic her new props,
she chatted uneasily, then easily
about Derrida, the revolution, her dry tongue
                                    flapping,
licked by someone else's words; she was undone.

Bio Logic

Alveoli, dirigibles of air
fall to shadows, ash memories. Some cells
will now breed mutant forms, disease that swells
to dark contagion. Fags, not bio weapons' glare,
still the serried cilia—once anemones—
and turn the gullet black.
                              The sputters cease
and let withered flapping forms' decay
regenerate in sputum that suckles
some with enzymes, breast puckers
gone, dissolved in a discarded ashtray.
Clear breath brings changes and melodies
haunt my reverie. The chest, hard-paced
and tumour-free, accepts my love's embrace
and seethes with passion like a squally sea.

Note from a Young Syrian
to His Cousin in Brighton

It's there—my artificial leg, I mean—
dumped in this shelled souk. Do tell my aunt
that this bazaar's not like your Churchill Square,
and I can no longer stroll and barter.

Once a footloose, night-hiking loiterer
who lived in mirages—a stargazer—
now I'll learn to hop, and when the earth lulls,
try to kick a football like your Seagulls,
but never walk to lemon-scented hills
and hear the luring echo of sheep bells,
nor pick pistachios and chew them raw.
The muezzin no longer calls to prayer,

and dreams of visiting you one day are dust;
it's not worked, we're out of the running, duds.

Sudoku in Costa Coffee

She kept a record in a jotter with pink hearts
of her sudoku scores and crossword clues,
cross-referenced to try to find the answers.
Maybe it would provide a solution
to what had happened in her life,
to what she'd lost and where she had lost out.

Her dimpled fingers clutched a pencil stub,
but sometimes she would squeeze the empty air,
which made her look quite tame, but fazed;
her split hair frayed and coiffed,
like a young wife's should be: an Alice
band pinned down the greying strands.

She flicked her red top open at page three,
then moved on to the centre spread, a scandal
of the drunken star who'd smashed his car,
then beat his girlfriend, left her pale and hurt,
yet there she was, spreadeagled on a bed,
flashing her tawdry undies, with a smile.

Ignored by Chinese undergrad baristas,
she caught the eye of older men who'd snort
and look away: the *cast-off wife*.
She still sudokued as I left,
my brow buried in a feminist
poem and bent against the rain.

The Counsellor

They kissed a sonnet ago, in verse. The free
and single world derided it, and placed
their pale-bud bodies in moot enquiry:
the breakups, fights and battered
briefs to barristers: be kind to me.

When the dawn broke, turned black,
then back into a daytime nightmare,
panic drilled deep veins into her pain.
The macho strut of Matissian dancing done,
dead cries of decree nisi disrupted
the coitus interruptus forever,
and all the hubris that festered there.

The mindful counsellor says, you look all in,
and touches her, the child within.

Buff-tailed Bumblebee

A Sussex bee with coal-black face and tiger
stripe, nestling in juicy wheat fields in a heat,
takes flight and sips the pale-pink bud
of the broad bean's flowering pod.

In a dip over downland heather,
it finds the feathery relief of ferns
and nestles for another nettled hour
in a place of clouds and shelter.

It alights, buff tail fluttering,
on a round-headed rampion,
and nips its nectar, and the purple clover's,
dense in a thorny thicket copse.

The apiarian aeronaut alights
on spongy sphagnum, orchids,
the silver daisy flower
and the bramble briar rose.

Skimming over early blackberries
on the South Downs Way, it buzzes
in a noisy, fractious way, and ends its journey
between elderberries and bliss.

Alienation

«Я вернулся в мой город, знакомый до слез,
До прожилок, до детских припухлых желез.»

—*from 'Leningrad' by Osip Mandelstam*

I have been surprised into feeling,
seeing you standing casually at my open door.
I am uncertain it has happened,
and now I inhabit an alien place,
my homely life hostile to me.

The snows of February have been replaced
by a glaring March sun,
a sun that's preternatural, unkind
and out of place.

My boggy walks across the Downs
lack meaning—simply to escape
Brighton and its cliques.

I *do* remember Islington, and living with you
in a luxury of books and closeness,
and I liked the darkness of our house,

the smoggy light, the sound of traffic
and the non-rustle of wind in the non-trees.

Yes, sometimes one yearns for the capital,
for a life of cosmopolitan café debate;
the bourgeois luxuriating in wine
and intense nights.

I find life cold here,
like Mandelstam
did in Voronezh,
and am an alien, an exile,
though London is only an hour away
with you…

Jung, and Reincarnation

The ancestors, strange archetypal
beings that inhabit the arcane
recesses of the psyche, surfaced
—hungry Neolithic oddities—
and some of these personalities
looked uncannily like my mother.
Then someone said, my daughter
has disappointed me by not reading
out her piece. There were myriads
of mothers and daughters,
and I realised they were the shell people
of my unconscious.
And all this brought to mind strange thoughts
that I had had on metempsychosis
as a six-year-old,
for every evening my mother
would stand me on a yellow wooden chair
to reach up to the washbasin,
and while she flannelled me,
I would confide in her my thoughts
on reincarnation.
They were not dissimilar to Buddhist
ideas of rebirth.

Thus, if I were a goody-goody
I would meld in heaven
with a Blake-like god;
if half-and-half *sage* my afterlife
would be spent in the realm
of the mermaids
(my favourite fate,
because I could be wilful
without a telling-off);
if unruly, be sent to limbo,
a sphere wherein I'd float
freely and forever in space;
but if an out-and-out villain,
go to hell!
Nevertheless, these ideas
must have come from some
sort of collective unconscious,
for my true fate, I believed,
was to become a rose,
a stone, or even a fly,
endlessly changing,
dying and being reborn.

This is Where I Shelter

I think of Meg and Lucy—and Emily in Amherst
—and sense their presence in the rocks and trees:
things small, confined, unseen,
—unnoticed—a tracery of nothings.

It makes me muse on old Meg and her fate,
seen savouring swart blackberries,
the liquor dribbling down her chin,
but dead sometime under the brown heath turf.

Her skin and torso rot through moons,
and inside Meg's warm, hollow heart
a rust-red, grey-capped chaffinch builds its nest
and trills more lustily than the other birds.

And poor Lucy, too, has no refuge,
as I have often been bereft,
for in a silent room—dust motes on the half-open
slatted blinds, and the sun-struck furniture

offering respite to a false widow spider—
my mind has held me a prisoner,
pricked and goaded by nettling ideas.
I climb up to my single, top-floor room,

where I am marginally free to seek shelter,
for the little gnats, like me, retreat to the attic—
but for the indigent, a cardboard box
on a wet pavement is their asylum.

One Small Mistake

It's not a crime to make one small mistake:
you wed and then divorce, it's no great loss,
what matters is—be strong, be true—don't break.

You've drifted, failed tests, sat the retakes—
hay fever, sunshine is a time to snooze:
it's not the end to make a few mistakes.

You eructate then retch with visceral aches:
you've chosen *crème brûlée*, not fine lime sauce.
What matters is—have fun—eat gorgeous cakes!

I've let my son run free, miss the school intake:
the head looks black and pens an absent cross.
It's not a crime to make this small mistake.

I've lost a house, my reputation twice: my brake
on the thought's processes and crazy course.
What matters is—be strong, be true—don't break.

Be philosophical, present, mind awake,
no sycophancy, DO defy your boss,
I see it *is* the end—a small mistake!
What matters is: be strong, be true, and do not
                                        break.

Romance

I am—yet what I am, none cares or knows…as are all the marginalised people in the world, shunned, neglected and snared in voices. Tell them to read about witch hunts and bedlams. Then they will see and I will shout not to cast the first stone.

O rose, thou art sick…troubled and dying with an eighteenth-century disease; red wounds, like ruby lips, hissing the swollen grey flesh tubercular. There are lesions in this, my troubled language.

So, we'll go no more a roving, So late into the night… read at my father's funeral, prodigious, a vacancy. It plunges me into total grief. In sorrow, I can be mad and tender, but I am always alone.

Thou still unravished bride of quietness…this is how I feel: my still centre rests unique, original and untried. It cocoons my aesthetic spirit, and without this, my life would have been empty.

I *am* a Romantic like the poets: I am not romantic.
I covet black cloaks and wings. I yearn to be
a highwaywoman. How many poems have I
inhabited in my dreams?

This is who I am

Rape

I am sitting in the annexe of a church with my
hands interlocked and a supplicant on either side
of me. A woman with a fluty voice chants: God,
grant me the serenity to…and we all say with her:
to accept the things I cannot change. A lull makes
me blush, cough and break the clinging film of
peace, but a voice breaks into a tale about a brother
in prison, the wind-burnt face telling us about his
life on the deep streets. He plays a violin and says it's
saved his life. Another confesses, whimsically—her
child has been snatched away, but she'll get her back
soon. Then another. They all have their stories, but
do I have one? Some stories are subterranean. Am
I even abstinent? I feel intoxicated. I can't say it's all
checked out. Try to recollect…
—Men jag älskar min lilla flycka!
—Natt natt, Mamma, natt natt…
The square of shimmering light from the small
window casts moving shadows on my starry
ceiling from the crepuscule. I lie listening to voices
creeping upwards, past the *Sverige* arras map on the
timbered staircase imprinted with Öland windmills
darned in wool, Småland lakes in cyan ribbon, and

44

red-stitched Dala horses with pricked ears prancing
across two latitudes. It is deepening in me—a
notion of *pietas* for the voices—a universe before
words—of light and dark, wet and dry, grief and
waves, in a Kristevan, semiotic world.

Polis, polis, potatisgris! Mamma
is driving at a hundred miles an hour down an empty
motorway. My sister and I are happy, never so happy,
singing in the back seat: land of the silver birch, home
of the beaver, where still the mighty moose wanders
at will, blue lake and rocky shore, we will return once
more, while *Mamma* winds down the window and
screams into the wind, police, police potato pig, in
her native Swedish, and we pull faces at the people
in the car behind. It is a crazy and daring thing to
do, but she always says funny things and I never stop
laughing; driving away with my mother.

Tack så mycket. Jag tycker om pyttipanna till frukost
Here I am, in a straw hat and cherry-pink uniform,
being taught Catullus, but not Sappho, an extravagance
beyond the school budget—or closer to the bone,
girls are never taught Greek. Suffering and in love
with my Latin teacher, with her tight dark bun,

white broderie anglaise-trimmed smock to conceal
chalk dust, and neat legs, I often imagine I catch her
eye and she has singled me out to be her special child.
Those anecdotes about Roman poets' transgressive
lives—the little sparrow gets everywhere.

Jag äter nyponsoppa och kroppkakor till kvällsmat.
Tack, tack, Mormor
Always alone, I make the weary train journey
home, trying to force my eyes to stay open to read
-isms—feminism, Marxism. Home for tea is a long
hour away, *och*—homework till late.

No Swedish spoken here
In the bedsit downtown, a bearded man I've met
earlier at a political rally—met, but barely know—
with his trade union official badges on his lapel and
stained brown fingers from reefers and beer, picks
me apart stitch by stitch. I know—always rather
knowing and precocious they say, in school reports—
that it is statutory rape, and that my carefree
classmates will never seem the same again, as I gaze
back to the drowning schoolroom, the intricate
smock floating away on the surface of the water like
a white sail, resembling a boat bound for Carthage.

Les Fleurs du mal...

I am fat but have no weight in the world. School dropout drifting, travelling, I kiss the boy on the ferry train. Reading my pocket book of French poetry in a flat—the HLM—in south-east France, I discover Rimbaud and Baudelaire. I climb the Vercors Massif and see Ophelia rise from her watery grave and the snow queen in her icy hall. I have drunk the tainted mead.

Ja visst, jag älskar er, Mamma och Mormor
The soot-blackened windows of the Little Preston Street hall are darkening, and the meeting is nearly ended. A few more say their bit. *Jävla flicka*—damn girl—where did I hear this? Is it those voices that have come into my head lately? You're being stitched up. No, you're being hemmed together again. You're a nursed, fussy and cared for thing. Am I? *Ja visst!*—memories of a Swedish grandmother. She smiles and hands me a cardigan she has knitted for me. *Tack så mycket för allt, Mormor och Mamma.*
God natt!

Notes on the text

Memories of a Swedish Grandmother

'Mormor' is the Swedish word for grandmother, specifically 'mother's mother'. If it was father's mother, the word would be *'farmor'*. Winter's festival of light is Santa Lucia, on 13th December, and one of the main festivals in Sweden. 'Sill' is pickled herring and eaten a lot in Sweden, and dill is one of the most commonly used herbs in Sweden.

Pastoral

Comus is a masque in honour of chastity, and was written by John Milton. Known colloquially as *Comus*, the masque's actual full title is: *A Masque presented at Ludlow Castle, 1634, on Michaelmas night, before the Right Honourable John, Earl of Bridgewater, Viscount Brackly, Lord President of Wales, and one of His Majesty's most honourable Privy Council.*

The Gift

Linnea Borealis, or Twinflower, are pink bell-like fragrant flowers that grow in pairs. The Linnea

Borealis is the unofficial national flower of the Kingdom of Sweden.

Women Sewing

This is a poem from my Creative Writing MA. It is in the voice of a Russian girl living in the 1930s in a small, provincial town called Saransk. The semiotician Mikhail Mikhailovich Bakhtin was exiled to this town by Stalin.

Romance

I am—yet what I am, none cares or knows
— from 'I Am!' John Clare, 1848

O rose, thou art sick
—from 'The Sick Rose', William Blake, 1794

So, we'll go no more a roving, So late into the night
—from 'So We'll Go No More a Roving',
Lord George Byron, 1817

Thou still unravished bride of quietness
—from 'Ode on a Grecian Urn', John Keats, 1820

Rape

Men jag älskar min lilla flycka!
Natt natt, Mamma, natt natt…
But I love my little girl!
Night night, Mum, night night…

Polis, polis, potatisgris
In Sweden there's a law against calling policemen
pigs, because of the popular rhyme *polis, polis,*
potatisgris (police, police, potato pig).

Tack så mycket. Jag tycker om pyttipanna till frukost
Pyttipanna is a hotchpotch of food, a Swedish
term meaning 'small pieces in pan'. I remember
leftover roast meat, potatoes, lingonberry jam,
smoked bacon, carrots, onions, beetroot and other
ingredients. We ate it for breakfast (*frukost*).

Jag äter nyponsoppa och kroppkakor till kvällsmat.
I eat rosehip soup and potato dumplings for supper—
both these things taste very good!

Ja visst, jag älskar er, Mamma och Mormor
Yes, of course I love you, Mum and Grandma.

Acknowledgements

I would like to thank, with warmth and appreciation, the people and organisations who helped me with my poetry: Creative Future, who had faith enough in my writing to enable me to be published; Myriad Editions, in particular Candida Lacey and Victoria Heath Silk, for their professional guidance; New Writing South, who provided me with my mentors; John McCullough and Claudia Gould, for their early reading, encouragement and wonderful advice about my poems; Brighton Poetry Stanza who, in the past, offered me friendship, read and critiqued my work, and encouraged me to carry on writing. I have very happy memories of monthly evening meetings in the Green Room at The Brunswick in Hove, led by Jo Grigg. And finally, thanks to Dad, Mum, Jane, Tom, and the twins, for all their love.

About the author

Sarah Windebank has an English father and Swedish mother. She has degrees from University College London and the University of Sussex, and has taught English Literature and Language in China and the UK. She lives in Brighton.

About Spotlight

Spotlight Books is a collaboration between Myriad Editions, Creative Future and New Writing South to discover, guide and support writers whose voices are under-represented.

Our aim is to spotlight new talent that otherwise would not be recognised, and to help writers who face barriers, or lack opportunities, to develop their creative and professional skills in order to create a lasting legacy of work.

Each of our three organisations is dedicated to specific aspects of writer development. Together we are able to offer a clear ladder of support, from mentorship through to development editing and promotional opportunities.

Spotlight books are not only treasures in themselves but also beacons to other under-represented writers. For further information, please visit: www.creativefuture.org.uk

Spotlight is supported by Arts Council England.

'These works are both nourishing and inspiring, and a gift to any reader.'—Kerry Hudson

Spotlight stories

Georgina Aboud
Cora Vincent

Tara Gould
The Haunting of Strawberry Water

Ana Tewson-Božić
Crumbs

Spotlight poetry

Jacqueline Haskell
Stroking Cerberus: Poems from the Afterlife

Elizabeth Ridout
Summon

Sarah Windebank
Memories of a Swedish Grandmother